Brew Your Own Beer

DIY Brewing Beer At Home: Brew Your Own Beer, Dammit

That Beer Guy

Published by Chilling Press, 2024.

DIY BREWING BEER AT HOME: BREW YOUR OWN BEER, DAMMIT

First edition. April 5, 2024.

Copyright © 2024 That Beer Guy.

ISBN: 979-8224933822

Written by That Beer Guy.

Table of Contents

Chapter 1

Part 1: Understanding Ingredients

Homebrewing, as an art form and a science, necessitates a comprehensive understanding of the core constituents that collectively give rise to the diverse range of flavors, aromas, colors, and textures found in beer. These primary ingredients, namely malt, hops, yeast, and water, serve as the foundational building blocks upon which the brewer's creativity and expertise are built. By delving into the intricate nuances of each component, homebrewers can unlock a world of possibilities, allowing them to craft beers that are not only delicious but also reflective of their unique vision and preferences.

1. Malt: The Soul of Beer

Malt, derived primarily from barley grains, serves as the backbone of beer, providing the fermentable sugars necessary for the alchemy of fermentation to occur. However, its significance extends far beyond mere sugar content, as it contributes a myriad of flavors, colors, and mouthfeel characteristics to the finished brew. The malting process involves steeping barley in water, allowing it to germinate, and then halting germination through kilning. This results in the development of enzymes that convert starches into fermentable sugars, as well as the formation of a diverse array of flavor compounds.

Within the realm of malt lies a vast spectrum of possibilities, ranging from the pale, biscuity sweetness of Pilsner malt to the rich, roasty complexity of chocolate malt. Crystal malts, with their caramelized sugars and toffee-like sweetness, add depth and richness to beers, while specialty malts such as Munich and Vienna contribute distinct nutty, bready, or biscuity notes. By carefully selecting and blending different malt varieties, brewers can tailor their recipes to achieve specific flavor profiles, whether it be the malty richness of a traditional Märzen or the roasty bitterness of an imperial stout.

2. Hops: The Spice of Beer

Hops, the flowering cones of the Humulus lupulus plant, serve as the aromatic and bittering agents in beer, imparting a multitude of flavors and aromas that range from floral and citrusy to herbal and piney. Beyond their sensory contributions, hops also play a critical role in balancing the sweetness of malt and acting as a natural preservative, inhibiting the growth of harmful bacteria and extending the shelf life of the finished product.

The flavor and aroma characteristics of hops are influenced by factors such as variety, growing conditions, and processing methods. Some hop varieties, such as Cascade and Centennial, are prized for their bright, citrusy aromas, while others, like Saaz and Hallertau, offer delicate floral and herbal notes.

Additionally, hops can be added at different stages of the brewing process—whether it be during the boil for bitterness, in the whirlpool for aroma, or during dry-hopping for a burst of fresh hop character. Through experimentation with hop varieties and techniques, brewers can craft beers that showcase a diverse range of hop profiles, from the assertive bitterness of an IPA to the subtle, nuanced aromas of a Belgian farmhouse ale.

3. Yeast:

The Catalyst of Fermentation Yeast, often referred to as the unsung hero of brewing, is responsible for the transformative process of fermentation, wherein sugars are converted into alcohol and carbon dioxide. Beyond its primary role in alcohol production, yeast also contributes significantly to the flavor, aroma, and mouthfeel of beer through the byproducts of fermentation, including esters, phenols, and higher alcohols.

There are two primary categories of yeast used in brewing: ale yeast and lager yeast. Ale yeast, which ferments at warmer temperatures (typically between 60°F and 75°F), tends to produce fruity, estery flavors and is associated with a wide range of beer styles, including ales, stouts, and porters. In contrast, lager yeast, which ferments at cooler temperatures (typically between 45°F and 55°F), produces clean, crisp flavors and is traditionally used in lager styles such as pilsners, Märzens, and Bocks.

Within each category, there exists a vast array of yeast strains, each with its own unique fermentation characteristics and flavor contributions. Some strains produce prominent banana or clove esters, characteristic of Belgian-style ales, while others produce clean, neutral flavors, ideal for showcasing the malt and hop profiles of a beer. By selecting the appropriate yeast strain and controlling fermentation conditions, brewers can exert a significant degree of control over the flavor profile and character of their beers, allowing for endless experimentation and innovation.

4. Water: The Essence of Life

Water, often overlooked but undeniably essential, serves as the primary solvent in brewing, facilitating the extraction of flavors from malt and hops and influencing the pH level of the wort throughout the brewing process. While water quality may vary depending on geographical location and source, its composition can profoundly impact the flavor, mouthfeel, and overall character of the finished beer.

Different styles of beer may require adjustments to water chemistry to achieve optimal brewing results. For example, the soft water of Pilsen, Czech Republic, is ideal for brewing delicate, crisp lagers such as Pilsners, while the carbonate-rich water of Burton upon Trent, England, is well-suited for brewing malty, hop-forward ales such as IPAs. Brewers may adjust water profiles through techniques such as dilution, filtration, or the addition of brewing salts, allowing them to tailor their water to specific beer styles and achieve desired brewing outcomes.

Furthermore, water quality plays a critical role in sanitation and hygiene throughout the brewing process, as any contaminants present in the water supply can potentially compromise the integrity of the final product. By understanding the composition of their water and implementing appropriate measures to ensure its purity, brewers can safeguard against off-flavors and microbial contamination, ensuring that their beers are of the highest quality and consistency.

By delving deeply into the complexities of these four primary ingredients—malt, hops, yeast, and water—homebrewers can gain a profound appreciation for the art and science of brewing, as well as the boundless creative possibilities that lie within their grasp. Armed with knowledge and experimentation, they can embark on a journey of exploration and discovery, crafting beers that not only satisfy the palate but also nourish the soul.

Part 2: Exploring Essential Equipment

Equipping oneself with the right tools is paramount for a successful homebrewing endeavor. From basic starter kits to more advanced setups, the selection and utilization of brewing equipment play a pivotal role in the brewing process. In this part of the chapter, we will explore the essential equipment needed for brewing beer at home, diving into each component's function, importance, and practical considerations.

1. Fermenters: The Heart of the Brewery

Fermenters, vessels in which wort is transformed into beer through fermentation, are the cornerstone of any brewing operation. These vessels come in various shapes, sizes, and materials, each with its own unique advantages and considerations. Plastic fermenters, such as food-grade buckets or carboys, are popular among beginner brewers due to their affordability, durability, and ease of use. However, they may be prone to scratching and harboring bacteria if not properly cleaned and sanitized. Glass carboys offer the advantage of being transparent, allowing brewers to monitor the fermentation process, but they can be heavy and fragile. Stainless steel fermenters are favored by more experienced brewers for their durability, ease of cleaning, and resistance to scratches and contamination. They also offer temperature control options, such as jacketed or insulated models, which can be beneficial for maintaining consistent fermentation conditions. Ultimately, the choice of fermenter depends on factors such as budget, space constraints, and personal preferences.

2. Brewing Kettles: Where the Magic Happens

Brewing kettles, also known as brew pots or boilers, serve as the stage upon which the brewing process unfolds. These vessels are used for heating water, boiling wort, and adding hops during the brewing process. When selecting a brewing kettle, it is essential to consider factors such as capacity, material, and features. Stainless steel kettles are favored for their durability, heat conductivity, and ease of cleaning. They come in various sizes, ranging from small stovetop models to large, commercial-grade kettles suitable for batch brewing. Some kettles feature built-in thermometers, sight glasses, and ball valves for precise temperature control and wort handling. Additionally, brewers may opt for kettles with tri-clad bottoms or induction-ready designs for efficient heat distribution and compatibility with different heat sources. Whichever kettle you choose, ensure that it is large enough to accommodate your batch size and equipped with the necessary accessories for a seamless brewing experience.

3. Mash Tuns: Unlocking the Power of Grain

Mash tuns are vessels used for mashing, the process of mixing crushed malt with hot water to convert starches into fermentable sugars. These vessels come in various configurations, including cooler-style mash tuns, insulated kettles, and dedicated mash tuns with false bottoms or screens. Cooler-style mash tuns, typically made of food-grade plastic or stainless steel, are popular among homebrewers for their affordability, insulation properties, and ease of assembly. They are equipped with a drainage system, such as a ball valve or spigot, for lautering (draining) the sweet wort from the spent grains. Insulated kettles, on the other hand, offer the advantage of built-in temperature control, allowing brewers to maintain mash temperatures within a narrow range for optimal enzymatic activity. Dedicated mash tuns with false bottoms or screens prevent grain particles from clogging the drainage system and ensure efficient lautering. Consider your budget, brewing setup, and batch size when choosing a mash tun that best suits your needs.

4. Chilling and Heating Systems: Keeping Temperatures in Check

Temperature control is critical at various stages of the brewing process, from mashing and boiling to fermenting and conditioning. Chilling and heating systems, such as immersion chillers, counterflow chillers, heat exchangers, and electric heating elements, provide brewers with the means to achieve and maintain precise temperature control throughout the brewing cycle. Immersion chillers, consisting of a coiled copper or stainless steel tube, are submerged in the wort and connected to a cold water source, rapidly cooling the wort to pitching temperature after boiling. Counterflow chillers utilize a similar principle but employ a double-walled design to increase surface area contact between the wort and cooling water, resulting in faster chilling times. Heat exchangers, commonly used in commercial breweries, transfer heat between two separate fluids, such as wort and glycol, through a series of plates or tubes. Electric heating elements, integrated into brewing kettles or fermentation vessels, allow brewers to precisely control the temperature of the brewing or fermentation process. By investing in a reliable chilling and heating system, brewers can ensure consistent results and minimize the risk of off-flavors caused by temperature fluctuations.

5. Hydrometers and Thermometers: Instruments of Precision

Hydrometers and thermometers are indispensable tools for monitoring and measuring various parameters throughout the brewing process. Hydrometers, also known as saccharometers or brewers' hydrometers, measure the specific gravity or density of wort before and after fermentation, allowing brewers to calculate the alcohol content and monitor fermentation progress. They consist of a weighted glass or plastic float calibrated to specific gravity readings, with a scale indicating the density of the liquid.

Thermometers, essential for monitoring mash and fermentation temperatures, come in various styles, including dial thermometers, digital thermometers, and infrared thermometers. Dial thermometers, inserted directly into the mash tun or kettle, provide accurate temperature readings within a specified range. Digital thermometers offer the convenience of instant temperature readings and programmable alarms for temperature control. Infrared thermometers, which use infrared technology to measure surface temperatures, are ideal for non-contact temperature measurements during fermentation or chilling. By regularly calibrating and using hydrometers and thermometers during the brewing process, brewers can ensure consistency, accuracy, and quality in their beer production.

6. Sanitation Tools: Maintaining Brewery Hygiene

Sanitation is paramount in brewing, as any contaminants present in the brewing environment can compromise the integrity of the final product. To maintain brewery hygiene and prevent microbial contamination, brewers utilize a variety of sanitation tools and chemicals, including cleaners, sanitizers, brushes, and spray bottles. Cleaners, such as oxygen-based cleaners or alkaline detergents, are used to remove organic residues, protein deposits, and other soil from brewing equipment and surfaces. Sanitizers, such as iodophor, chlorine dioxide, or acid-based sanitizers, are used to kill or inhibit the growth of bacteria, yeast, and mold on brewing equipment and packaging materials. Brushes, designed for specific tasks such as cleaning fermenters, kegs, or draft lines, help brewers reach and remove stubborn residues from hard-to-reach areas. Spray bottles, filled with sanitizer or diluted cleaning solution, are used to apply sanitizers to brewing equipment and surfaces, ensuring thorough coverage and contact time. By incorporating proper sanitation practices into their brewing routine, brewers can minimize the risk of off-flavors and microbial contamination, ensuring that their beers are safe, clean, and free from undesirable off-flavors.

By investing in quality equipment and maintaining proper brewing practices, homebrewers can create exceptional beers that rival their commercial counterparts in flavor, aroma, and quality. Whether brewing on a small scale or dreaming of scaling up to a larger operation, the right tools and techniques are essential for unlocking the full potential of one's brewing prowess and creativity. So, roll up your

Chapter 2

Part 1: A Journey Through Beer Styles

Beer is a beverage with a rich and diverse history, spanning cultures and continents, each contributing its own unique styles, traditions, and brewing techniques. From the crisp, refreshing lagers of Germany to the robust, complex ales of Belgium, the world of beer offers a kaleidoscope of flavors, aromas, and experiences for enthusiasts to explore and enjoy. In this part of the chapter, we embark on a journey through some of the most iconic and beloved beer styles, categorizing them into ale, lager, and hybrid categories, and uncovering the distinct characteristics that define each style.

1. Ale Styles:

Exploring Tradition and Innovation

Ale, one of the oldest and most diverse beer categories, encompasses a wide range of styles characterized by their use of top-fermenting yeast strains and warmer fermentation temperatures. From the fruity esters of Belgian Trappist ales to the robust roastiness of English stouts, ales offer a spectrum of flavors, colors, and aromas that cater to a variety of palates and preferences.

• Pale Ales and IPAs:

Pale ales and India Pale Ales (IPAs) are among the most popular and recognizable ale styles, known for their assertive hop bitterness, vibrant hop aromas, and pale to amber coloration. Pale ales typically exhibit a balanced malt-hop profile, with moderate bitterness and citrusy, floral hop aromas. IPAs, on the other hand, feature heightened hop bitterness and aroma, often showcasing bold, resinous, or tropical fruit flavors from American or New World hop varieties.

- Porters and Stouts:

Porters and stouts are dark, malty ales characterized by their roasted malt flavors, chocolatey undertones, and creamy mouthfeel. Porters tend to be lighter in body and flavor, with notes of caramel, toffee, and coffee, while stouts are richer and more robust, often featuring flavors of dark chocolate, espresso, and dried fruit. Variations such as oatmeal stouts, milk stouts, and imperial stouts offer further complexity and depth, making them popular choices for cold winter nights or dessert pairings.

- Belgian Ales:

Belgian ales, renowned for their complexity, yeast-driven flavors, and high carbonation levels, encompass a diverse range of styles, including Trappist ales, Abbey ales, and Saisons. Trappist ales, brewed by Trappist monasteries, are characterized by their fruity esters, spicy phenols, and malt-forward profiles, with variations such as Dubbels, Tripels, and Quadrupels offering increasing levels of strength and complexity. Abbey ales, brewed in the style of Trappist beers by non-Trappist breweries, often feature similar yeast characteristics but with greater variation in recipe and interpretation. Saisons, or farmhouse ales, are rustic, artisanal beers originally brewed by Belgian farmers for seasonal consumption, known for their dry, fruity, and peppery flavors, as well as their high carbonation levels.

2. Lager Styles:

Crisp, Clean, and Refreshing Lager, a beer category characterized by its use of bottom-fermenting yeast strains and cooler fermentation temperatures, encompasses a wide range of styles known for their crisp, clean, and refreshing characteristics. From the pale, golden hues of German Pilsners to the malty sweetness of Munich Dunkels, lagers offer a diverse array of flavors and profiles that appeal to a broad spectrum of beer drinkers.

• Pilsners:

Pilsner, the quintessential lager style, originated in the Czech city of Pilsen in the 19th century and quickly became one of the world's most popular beer styles. Known for its pale, golden color, firm bitterness, and crisp, dry finish, Pilsner showcases the noble hop varieties of Saaz and Tettnang, which impart floral, spicy, and herbal aromas. German-style Pilsners, with their slightly more pronounced bitterness and hop character, offer a refreshing alternative to their Czech counterparts.

• Helles and Dortmunder Export:

Helles, meaning "pale" in German, is a traditional Bavarian lager known for its smooth, malt-forward profile, balanced bitterness, and golden color. Featuring flavors of bread crust, honey, and light floral hops, Helles is a sessionable beer that pairs well with a variety of foods. Dortmunder Export, originating from the city of Dortmund in Germany, is a slightly stronger and more hop-forward lager style, with a pale to amber color and a crisp, clean finish.

• Vienna and Marzen:

Vienna Lager, developed in Vienna, Austria, in the 19th century, is characterized by its amber color, rich malt sweetness, and subtle hop bitterness. With flavors of toasted bread, caramel, and nutty undertones, Vienna Lager offers a balanced and approachable drinking experience. Märzen, or March beer, is a traditional German lager brewed in March and aged through the summer months for consumption during Oktoberfest celebrations. With its amber to copper color, malt-forward profile, and clean, dry finish, Märzen showcases flavors of caramel, toffee, and toasted grain.

3. Hybrid Styles: Blending Tradition with Innovation

Hybrid beer styles, often referred to as "cross-over" styles, combine elements of both ale and lager brewing techniques, resulting in beers that exhibit characteristics of both categories. These styles offer brewers a canvas for creativity and experimentation, allowing them to push the boundaries of tradition while maintaining respect for classic brewing techniques.

• California Common/Steam Beer:

California Common, also known as Steam Beer, is a uniquely American style that originated in California during the 19th century. Brewed with lager yeast but fermented at ale temperatures, California Common exhibits characteristics of both ale and lager styles. It typically features a medium to dark amber color, moderate hop bitterness, and a clean, crisp finish. The use of Northern Brewer hops imparts woody, minty, and piney aromas, while the signature "steam" character is achieved through a combination of fermentation temperature and yeast selection.

• Kölsch:

Kölsch is a traditional beer style from Cologne, Germany, known for its pale, straw-colored appearance, delicate malt sweetness, and subtle hop bitterness. Brewed with ale yeast but cold-conditioned like a lager, Kölsch offers a clean, crisp drinking experience with flavors of biscuit, bread crust, and a touch of fruity esters from fermentation. Traditionally served in cylindrical glasses called "Stange," Kölsch is a refreshing and sessionable beer that pairs well with a variety of foods.

• Cream Ale:

Cream Ale is an American beer style with roots dating back to the mid-19th century, characterized by its light golden color, mild malt sweetness, and subtle hop bitterness. Brewed with ale yeast but fermented at cooler temperatures, Cream Ale offers a clean, crisp drinking experience with flavors of corn, grain, and a hint of fruity esters.

It is often compared to American lagers for its smooth, easy-drinking character and is a popular choice for outdoor gatherings and social occasions.

• Altbier:

Altbier, meaning "old beer" in German, is a traditional ale style from the Rhineland region, known for its copper to dark brown color, balanced malt-hop profile, and clean, lager-like finish. Brewed with ale yeast but cold-conditioned like a lager, Altbier offers flavors of toasted bread, caramel, and floral hops, with a crisp, dry finish. It is often served in narrow glasses called "Stange" or "Altbier glasses" to showcase its rich malt character and subtle hop bitterness.

• Biere de Garde:

Biere de Garde, meaning "beer for keeping" in French, is a traditional farmhouse ale style from northern France, known for its amber to copper color, rich malt sweetness, and subtle fruity esters. Brewed with ale yeast but cold-conditioned like a lager, Biere de Garde offers flavors of caramel, toffee, and dark fruit, with a clean, dry finish. It is often aged for several months to develop complex, mellow flavors and is traditionally served in large, bulbous glasses called "tulip glasses."

Exploring these hybrid beer styles offers brewers a glimpse into the creative possibilities of blending tradition with innovation, resulting in beers that transcend categorization and offer unique drinking experiences for enthusiasts and novices alike.

As we journey through the diverse landscape of beer styles, it becomes evident that the world of beer is as vast and varied as the cultures and communities that produce it. From the crisp, clean lagers of Germany to the bold, complex ales of Belgium, each beer style tells a story of tradition, innovation, and craftsmanship, inviting us to savor and celebrate the rich tapestry of flavors, aromas, and experiences that beer has to offer. In the next part of the chapter, we will delve into the process of crafting our own signature brews, exploring the art and science of recipe development and experimentation.

Part 2: Crafting Your Own Signature Brew

Armed with knowledge about different beer styles, you're now ready to embark on the exciting journey of creating your own recipes. In this part of the chapter, we'll explore the process of recipe development, offering guidance on selecting ingredients, balancing flavors, and experimenting with brewing techniques to craft unique and personalized brews.

1. Understanding Flavor Profiles

Before diving into recipe development, it's essential to have a clear understanding of the flavor profile you want to achieve in your beer. Consider the characteristics of your favorite beer styles and the flavor preferences of yourself and your intended audience. Are you aiming for a hop-forward IPA with bold citrus and pine notes, or a malt-driven stout with rich chocolate and coffee flavors? Understanding the balance of malt sweetness, hop bitterness, yeast esters, and other flavor components will guide your ingredient selection and recipe formulation.

2. Selecting Ingredients

Once you've determined the flavor profile you want to achieve, it's time to select the ingredients that will bring your vision to life. Start with the base malt, choosing varieties that will provide the desired color, body, and maltiness for your beer style. Supplement the base malt with specialty malts to add complexity and depth, selecting varieties that contribute flavors and aromas complementary to your desired profile. For hoppy beers, choose hop varieties with the characteristics you're looking for, whether it's citrusy, floral, piney, or herbal. Experiment with different yeast strains to find one that enhances the desired flavors and fermentation characteristics of your beer. Additionally, consider adjuncts such as fruits, spices, and herbs to add unique flavors and aromas to your brew.

3. Balancing Flavors

Achieving balance is key to crafting a well-rounded and enjoyable beer. Pay attention to the ratio of malt sweetness to hop bitterness, ensuring that neither component overwhelms the other. Consider the perceived bitterness of the hops, as well as the residual sweetness of the malt, when calculating the bitterness units (IBUs) of your beer. Aim for a harmonious blend of flavors, with each component complementing and enhancing the others. Keep in mind that fermentation will also contribute flavors and aromas to the final beer, so select a yeast strain that will complement the desired profile and fermentation characteristics of your brew.

4. Experimenting with Techniques

Brewing is both an art and a science, and experimentation is key to pushing the boundaries of flavor and innovation. Don't be afraid to try new brewing techniques, such as different mashing schedules, hop additions, or fermentation temperatures, to achieve the desired results. Keep detailed notes of your brewing process, including ingredients, measurements, and observations, to track your progress and learn from each batch. Joining a homebrewing club or online community can also provide valuable feedback and inspiration for future brews.

5. Iterating and Refining

Like any creative endeavor, crafting the perfect beer recipe takes time, patience, and iteration. Don't be discouraged if your first batch doesn't turn out exactly as planned—use it as an opportunity to learn and refine your technique. Tweak your recipe with each iteration, adjusting ingredient quantities, brewing parameters, and fermentation conditions until you achieve the desired flavor profile and consistency. Remember that brewing is a journey, and each batch brings you one step closer to brewing your perfect beer.

By following these steps and embracing the spirit of experimentation and creativity, you can craft your own signature brews that reflect your unique taste preferences and brewing style. Whether you're a novice brewer or a seasoned veteran, the process of recipe development offers endless opportunities for exploration, discovery, and innovation. So gather your ingredients, fire up your kettle, and let your imagination run wild as you embark on the exhilarating journey of brewing your own beer.

Chapter 3

Part 1: The Brewing Process Demystified

Brewing beer at home is an exciting and rewarding endeavor that allows you to create delicious beverages tailored to your taste preferences. In this part of the chapter, we'll demystify the brewing process, breaking it down into its key steps and exploring each stage in detail.

1. Recipe Formulation: Crafting Your Vision

Every great beer starts with a well-crafted recipe. Whether you're following a tried-and-true formula or experimenting with your own creation, recipe formulation is the first step in the brewing process. Begin by selecting your desired beer style and determining the ingredients needed to achieve its characteristic flavors, aromas, and appearance. Consider the balance of malt, hops, yeast, and water, as well as any specialty ingredients or adjuncts you plan to incorporate. Use brewing software or online calculators to calculate the quantities of each ingredient needed to achieve your target gravity, bitterness, and color.

2. Mashing: Extracting Fermentable Sugars

Mashing is the process of mixing crushed malted grains with hot water to extract fermentable sugars, proteins, and other soluble compounds. This step activates the enzymes present in the malt, which convert starches into sugars, creating a sweet, malty liquid known as wort. The temperature and duration of the mash, known as the mash schedule, play a crucial role in determining the fermentability and body of the finished beer. A single-step infusion mash, where the entire grain bill is mashed at a single temperature, is suitable for most beer styles. However, more complex mash schedules, such as step mashing or decoction mashing, may be employed for certain styles to achieve specific flavor and mouthfeel characteristics.

3. Lautering: Separating Wort from Grains

Once the mash is complete, the next step is lautering, or separating the sweet wort from the spent grains. This is typically done using a lauter tun or mash tun equipped with a false bottom or manifold to filter out the grain husks and other solid particles. The wort is drained from the mash tun and collected in the brew kettle, while the spent grains are either discarded or repurposed for other uses, such as animal feed or compost. Lautering should be done slowly and gently to avoid compacting the grain bed and extracting unwanted tannins and astringent compounds from the husks.

4. Boiling: Extracting Bitterness and Flavor

Once the wort has been collected, it is brought to a vigorous boil in the brew kettle. The boiling process serves several purposes, including sterilizing the wort, isomerizing hop acids to extract bitterness, and driving off volatile compounds that contribute to off-flavors and aromas. During the boil, hops are added at various intervals to impart bitterness, flavor, and aroma to the finished beer. The length of the boil and the timing of hop additions depend on the desired characteristics of the beer style being brewed. After the boil is complete, the wort is rapidly cooled to pitching temperature to prepare for fermentation.

5. Cooling: Preparing for Fermentation

After the boil, it's crucial to rapidly cool the wort to the optimal temperature for fermentation. This is typically done using a wort chiller, which circulates cold water or a heat exchange fluid through a coil immersed in the wort. Rapid cooling helps to precipitate proteins and other haze-causing compounds, as well as to lock in the desired hop aromas and flavors. It also helps to minimize the risk of contamination by quickly lowering the wort to a temperature that is inhospitable to most microorganisms. Once the wort has been cooled to pitching temperature, it is transferred to a fermentation vessel and inoculated with yeast to begin the fermentation process.

6. Fermentation: Transforming Wort into Beer:

Fermentation is the magical process by which yeast converts fermentable sugars in the wort into alcohol and carbon dioxide, producing beer as a byproduct. The fermentation vessel, whether it's a carboy, bucket, or conical fermenter, provides a controlled environment for yeast to thrive, with factors such as temperature, oxygenation, and nutrient availability playing a crucial role in fermentation success. Fermentation typically occurs in two stages: primary fermentation, where the bulk of fermentation activity takes place, and secondary fermentation or conditioning, where the beer is allowed to mature and develop additional flavors and clarity.

7. Conditioning and Packaging:

Finishing Touches:

After fermentation is complete, the beer undergoes a period of conditioning to allow flavors to mellow and mature, and to clarify the beer by allowing yeast and other suspended particles to settle out. This can take place in the primary fermentation vessel or in a separate conditioning vessel, depending on the beer style and desired outcome. Once the beer has reached its desired flavor profile and clarity, it is ready for packaging. This can involve transferring the beer to kegs for draft consumption, or bottling it in glass or plastic bottles for carbonation and storage. Proper sanitation and packaging techniques are essential to ensure that the beer remains fresh and free from contamination during storage and consumption.

By understanding and mastering each step of the brewing process, you can create delicious and satisfying beers that showcase your creativity and skill as a brewer. Whether you're brewing simple ales or complex lagers, the principles of recipe formulation, mashing, boiling, cooling, fermentation, conditioning, and packaging remain the same, providing a solid foundation for your brewing endeavors. So roll up your sleeves, fire up your kettle, and get ready to brew some amazing beer!

Part 2: Advanced Brewing Techniques

In this part of the chapter, we'll delve into advanced brewing techniques that allow homebrewers to take their craft to the next level. From experimental ingredients to specialized equipment and innovative processes, these techniques offer opportunities for creativity, exploration, and refinement in the pursuit of exceptional beer.

1. Hop Bursting and Hop Stands: Maximizing Hop Flavor and Aroma

Hop bursting and hop stands are techniques used to maximize hop flavor and aroma in beer by adding a large quantity of hops late in the brewing process. Rather than focusing solely on bittering hops added during the boil, these techniques emphasize late hop additions or whirlpooling to extract the essential oils responsible for intense hop aroma and flavor. By adding hops at lower temperatures, such as during whirlpooling or post-boil, brewers can achieve a smoother bitterness and brighter hop character in their beers. Experiment with different hop varieties, quantities, and timing to dial in the desired hop profile for your brew.

2. Dry Hopping: Enhancing Aroma and Freshness

Dry hopping is a technique used to enhance the aroma and freshness of beer by adding hops directly to the fermenter during or after fermentation. This allows the volatile hop oils to infuse the beer with vibrant aromas of citrus, pine, floral, or tropical fruits without contributing significant bitterness. Dry hopping is commonly used in hop-forward styles such as IPAs, pale ales, and hazy NEIPAs to boost aroma and perceived hop intensity. Experiment with different hop varieties and quantities to achieve the desired level of aroma and complexity in your beers.

3. Temperature Control and Fermentation Management

Temperature control is a critical aspect of fermentation management, as it directly influences yeast activity, fermentation kinetics, and the flavor profile of the finished beer. Advanced brewers invest in temperature-controlled fermentation chambers or glycol cooling systems to maintain precise fermentation temperatures throughout the brewing process. By controlling fermentation temperature, brewers can minimize off-flavors, reduce ester production, and ensure consistent fermentation performance across different yeast strains and beer styles. Additionally, temperature-controlled fermentation allows for the production of clean, well-attenuated beers with balanced flavors and aromas.

4. Yeast Management and Propagation

Yeast management and propagation techniques allow brewers to optimize yeast health, vitality, and performance for each brewing batch. Advanced brewers may harvest and repitch yeast from previous batches, propagate yeast cultures using laboratory-grade equipment, or experiment with mixed-culture fermentations using a combination of yeast and bacteria strains. By maintaining healthy yeast populations and minimizing stress during fermentation, brewers can achieve consistent fermentation results, improve beer stability, and enhance the overall quality of their brews. Experiment with different yeast strains, fermentation schedules, and pitching rates to explore the impact of yeast on beer flavor, aroma, and mouthfeel.

5. Barrel Aging and Wood Conditioning

Barrel aging and wood conditioning are techniques used to impart unique flavors, aromas, and textures to beer by aging it in wooden barrels or conditioning it with wood adjuncts such as chips, staves, or spirals. Barrel aging allows beer to interact with the wood, absorbing flavors and aromas such as vanilla, oak, coconut, and caramel from the barrel itself. Additionally, wood conditioning can contribute tannins, phenols, and other compounds that enhance complexity and mouthfeel in beer. Experiment with different types of barrels (e.g., bourbon, wine, rum) and wood varieties (e.g., oak, cherry, maple) to create distinctive and memorable barrel-aged beers.

By exploring these advanced brewing techniques, homebrewers can unlock new dimensions of flavor, aroma, and complexity in their beers. Whether it's maximizing hop character, mastering fermentation control, or experimenting with wood aging, there's always something new to discover and refine in the world of homebrewing. So roll up your sleeves, embrace the spirit of experimentation, and elevate your brewing game to new heights!

Chapter 4

Part 1: Troubleshooting and Problem-Solving in Homebrewing

While homebrewing can be a rewarding and enjoyable hobby, it's not without its challenges. In this part of the chapter, we'll explore common issues and pitfalls encountered by homebrewers and provide guidance on troubleshooting and problem-solving to ensure a successful brewing experience.

1. Off-Flavors and Aromas:

Identifying and Addressing Common Issues

Off-flavors and aromas can detract from the overall enjoyment of a beer and may indicate underlying issues in the brewing process. By familiarizing yourself with the most common off-flavors and their causes, you can quickly diagnose problems and take corrective action to improve your brews.

• Diacetyl:

Diacetyl is a buttery or butterscotch-like off-flavor that can result from incomplete fermentation or bacterial contamination. To address diacetyl, ensure a healthy and vigorous fermentation, and consider extending the conditioning phase to allow yeast to clean up any remaining diacetyl precursors.

• Acetaldehyde:

Acetaldehyde is a green apple-like off-flavor that can result from incomplete fermentation, oxidation, or bacterial contamination. To address acetaldehyde, ensure proper yeast pitching rates, adequate oxygenation of the wort, and minimize exposure to oxygen during transfer and packaging.

- Phenolic Off-Flavors:

Phenolic off-flavors, characterized by medicinal, band-aid, or clove-like aromas, can result from the presence of phenols produced by yeast or bacterial contamination. To address phenolic off-flavors, ensure proper yeast health and sanitation practices, and avoid using chlorine-based sanitizers, which can react with phenols to produce off-flavors.

- DMS (Dimethyl Sulfide):

DMS is a sulfur-like off-flavor reminiscent of cooked corn or cabbage and can result from insufficient boiling or bacterial contamination. To address DMS, ensure a vigorous boil, extend the boiling time for worts with high levels of DMS precursors, and practice proper sanitation to prevent bacterial contamination.

- Oxidation:

Oxidation can result in stale, cardboard-like flavors and aromas and is often caused by excessive exposure to oxygen during brewing, transfer, or packaging. To address oxidation, minimize splashing and agitation during transfer, purge packaging vessels with CO_2, and store finished beer in oxygen-impermeable containers.

2. Infection and Contamination:

Preventing and Mitigating Risks

Infection and contamination can result in off-flavors, off-odors, or even spoiled beer, posing a significant risk to the quality and safety of your brews. By implementing rigorous sanitation practices and maintaining a clean brewing environment, you can reduce the risk of infection and contamination and ensure the integrity of your beer.

- Cleaning and Sanitizing:

Proper cleaning and sanitizing of brewing equipment, fermenters, and packaging materials are essential to prevent microbial contamination. Use brewery-approved cleaners and sanitizers, follow recommended contact times and concentrations, and pay particular attention to hard-to-reach areas where bacteria and wild yeast can proliferate.

- Yeast Health and Propagation:

Healthy yeast is essential for a successful fermentation and can outcompete undesirable microorganisms that may cause infection or contamination. Ensure proper yeast handling, storage, and propagation techniques, use fresh yeast with high viability and vitality, and avoid pitching yeast into wort with residual sanitizer or cleaning agents.

- Fermentation Control:

Maintaining precise fermentation temperatures and conditions is crucial to preventing off-flavors and ensuring a clean fermentation. Use temperature-controlled fermentation chambers or cooling systems to regulate fermentation temperatures within the optimal range for your yeast strain, and monitor fermentation progress regularly to detect any signs of infection or contamination.

3. Stuck Fermentation and Under-Attenuation:

Resolving Fermentation Issues

Stuck fermentation and under-attenuation occur when yeast fail to ferment wort sugars completely, resulting in sweet, undercarbonated, or low-alcohol beers. By identifying the underlying causes of these issues and taking appropriate corrective action, you can salvage stalled fermentations and achieve the desired final gravity and flavor profile in your beers.

- Yeast Health and Pitching Rates:

Ensure proper yeast health and pitching rates by using fresh, viable yeast cultures and calculating the appropriate pitching rate based on the gravity and volume of your wort. Underpitching or pitching old yeast can lead to sluggish or incomplete fermentations, while overpitching can result in premature yeast flocculation and reduced attenuation.

- Fermentation Temperature:

Maintain stable fermentation temperatures within the optimal range for your yeast strain to ensure healthy yeast activity and complete attenuation. Fluctuations in temperature can stress yeast and inhibit fermentation, leading to stuck fermentations or incomplete attenuation.

- Nutrient Availability:

Ensure adequate nutrient availability for yeast by using yeast nutrient supplements or yeast starters, particularly in high-gravity or high-adjunct worts. Yeast require essential nutrients such as nitrogen, vitamins, and minerals for healthy cell growth and fermentation activity.

- Oxygenation and Aeration:

Properly oxygenate your wort before pitching yeast to ensure sufficient oxygen levels for healthy fermentation. Inadequate oxygenation can lead to sluggish or stuck fermentations, particularly in high-gravity worts or when using yeast strains with high oxygen requirements.

By understanding and addressing common issues and challenges in homebrewing, you can improve the quality and consistency of your beers and enjoy a more satisfying brewing experience. Whether it's diagnosing off-flavors, preventing contamination, or troubleshooting fermentation issues, proactive problem-solving is essential to mastering the art and science of homebrewing. So stay vigilant, stay curious, and never stop learning as you continue on your brewing journey.

Part 2: Scaling Up and Experimenting with Advanced Techniques

In this part of the chapter, we'll explore how homebrewers can scale up their operations and experiment with advanced brewing techniques to expand their horizons and push the boundaries of their craft.

1. Scaling Up:

Transitioning to Larger Batches:

As homebrewers gain experience and confidence in their brewing skills, many may choose to scale up their operations to brew larger batches of beer. Scaling up allows brewers to increase their production capacity, experiment with new recipes and techniques, and share their creations with a wider audience.

• Equipment Upgrades:

Scaling up often requires investing in larger brewing equipment, such as larger kettles, fermenters, and brewing systems. Consider upgrading your brewing setup gradually, starting with the most essential equipment and expanding as needed to accommodate larger batch sizes.

• Process Optimization:

With larger batches, process efficiency becomes increasingly important to ensure consistent results and minimize waste. Streamline your brewing process, optimize your workflow, and implement best practices for cleaning, sanitizing, and equipment maintenance to maximize efficiency and productivity.

• Recipe Adaptation:

When scaling up recipes from small to large batches, it's essential to consider factors such as ingredient proportions, hop utilization, and fermentation kinetics to maintain the desired flavor profile and balance. Use brewing software or online calculators to adjust ingredient quantities and brewing parameters accordingly.

• Quality Control:

As batch sizes increase, maintaining quality becomes paramount to ensuring the integrity and consistency of your beers. Implement quality control measures such as sensory evaluation, gravity and pH measurements, and microbiological testing to monitor fermentation progress, detect off-flavors, and identify areas for improvement.

2. Advanced Techniques:

Exploring New Frontiers:

With a solid foundation in brewing fundamentals, homebrewers can begin to explore advanced techniques and experimental brewing practices to push the boundaries of their craft and create truly unique and innovative beers.

• Wild and Mixed-Fermentation Beers:

Experiment with wild and mixed fermentation techniques to introduce complex and unpredictable flavors and aromas to your beers. Use a variety of yeast and bacteria strains, including wild or indigenous cultures, to ferment your wort and age your beer in oak barrels or other wooden vessels to develop sour, funky, and vinous characteristics.

• Brettanomyces and Funky Fermentations:

Embrace the funk with Brettanomyces, a wild yeast strain known for its distinctive barnyard, horse blanket, and tropical fruit aromas. Experiment with Brettanomyces fermentation in primary or secondary, as well as co-fermentation with other yeast strains to create complex and dynamic flavor profiles in your beers.

• Barrel Aging and Blending:

Explore the art of barrel aging and blending to create nuanced and sophisticated beers with layers of flavor and complexity. Age your beer in oak barrels previously used for spirits, wine, or other fermented beverages to impart unique wood-derived flavors and aromas. Experiment with blending different barrel-aged beers to achieve the desired balance and character.

• Alternative Ingredients and Adjuncts:

Think outside the box and experiment with alternative ingredients and adjuncts to add depth and complexity to your beers. Consider incorporating fruits, spices, herbs, flowers, coffee, chocolate, or even unconventional ingredients like seaweed, mushrooms, or edible flowers to create innovative and intriguing flavor combinations.

• Collaborations and Community:

Collaborate with other homebrewers, professional brewers, and local artisans to exchange ideas, share resources, and collaborate on brewing projects. Join homebrew clubs, attend brewing events and festivals, and participate in competitions to connect with fellow enthusiasts and gain inspiration for your brewing endeavors.

By scaling up their operations and experimenting with advanced techniques, homebrewers can take their craft to new heights and unlock a world of creativity and innovation. Whether it's brewing larger batches, exploring wild fermentation, or pushing the boundaries of flavor and style, the possibilities are endless for those willing to embrace the challenges and rewards of advanced homebrewing. So raise a glass to your brewing journey and toast to the endless possibilities that lie ahead!

Chapter 5

Part 1: Beer Styles Around the World

In this part of the chapter, we'll embark on a journey around the globe to explore the rich diversity of beer styles found in different regions and cultures. From the traditional brews of Europe to the innovative creations of the Americas and beyond, each beer style tells a story of history, culture, and craftsmanship.

1. Belgium:

Trappist Ales and Abbey Beers:

Belgium is renowned for its distinctive and diverse array of beer styles, many of which are brewed by Trappist monasteries and abbey breweries with centuries-old traditions. Trappist ales, such as Dubbel, Tripel, and Quadrupel, are characterized by their rich maltiness, fruity esters, and complex yeast-driven flavors. These beers are often brewed with candi sugar and undergo secondary fermentation in the bottle to achieve high carbonation and additional depth of flavor. Abbey beers, inspired by the brewing traditions of Trappist monasteries, encompass a wide range of styles, from Abbey Dubbels and Tripels to Blonde ales and Strong Dark ales, each with its own unique character and heritage.

2. Germany:

Pilsners, Weissbiers, and Bocks:

Germany is synonymous with beer culture, boasting a proud brewing tradition that dates back centuries. Pilsner, a pale, hoppy lager originating from the city of Pilsen in the Czech Republic, is one of the most popular beer styles in Germany and is known for its crisp, clean flavor and pronounced hop bitterness. Weissbier, or wheat beer, is another iconic German style, brewed with a significant proportion of malted wheat to impart a soft, creamy texture and distinctive banana and clove aromas. Bocks, including Maibock, Doppelbock, and Eisbock, are strong, malty lagers with robust flavors of caramel, toast, and dark fruit, traditionally brewed for special occasions and festivals.

3. United Kingdom:

Ales, Porters, and Stouts:

The United Kingdom has a rich brewing heritage dating back centuries, with ales, porters, and stouts among its most iconic beer styles. British ales, including Bitters, Pale Ales, and ESBs (Extra Special Bitters), are characterized by their balanced malt-hop profile, fruity yeast esters, and subtle bitterness. Porters, originally brewed in London during the 18th century, are dark, malty ales with flavors of roasted coffee, chocolate, and caramel. Stouts, a stronger and more robust version of porter, come in various sub-styles such as Dry Stout, Sweet Stout, and Imperial Stout, each offering its own interpretation of the rich, dark ale tradition.

4. United States:

IPAs, Pale Ales, and Barrel-Aged Beers:

The craft beer revolution in the United States has led to an explosion of creativity and innovation, with American brewers pushing the boundaries of beer styles and flavors. IPAs (India Pale Ales) are one of the most popular and influential beer styles in the modern craft beer movement, characterized by their bold hop aroma, high bitterness, and tropical fruit flavors. Pale Ales, including American Pale Ale and American Amber Ale, offer a more balanced and approachable alternative to IPAs, with moderate hop bitterness and caramel malt sweetness. Barrel-aged beers, such as Barrel-Aged Stouts, Sours, and Barleywines, have become increasingly popular among craft brewers, who age their beers in whiskey, bourbon, wine, or rum barrels to impart unique flavors and aromas.

5. Other Regions:

Lambics, Saisons, and Beyond:

Beyond the traditional beer-producing regions of Europe and North America, a diverse array of beer styles can be found in other parts of the world. Belgian Lambics, spontaneously fermented sour ales brewed in the Senne River valley, are known for their tart, funky flavors and complex microbial character. Saisons, or farmhouse ales, originated in the French-speaking regions of Belgium and France and are characterized by their fruity yeast esters, spicy phenols, and dry, refreshing finish. Other regions, such as Scandinavia, South America, and Asia, are also making their mark on the global beer scene with unique and innovative beer styles that reflect their local ingredients, traditions, and cultures.

As we journey through the diverse landscape of beer styles around the world, it becomes evident that beer is much more than just a beverage—it's a reflection of history, culture, and creativity. Each beer style tells a story of tradition, innovation, and craftsmanship, inviting us to savor and celebrate the rich tapestry of flavors, aromas, and experiences that beer has to offer. In the next part of the chapter, we'll explore the art of beer and food pairing, discovering how different beer styles can complement and enhance a wide range of culinary delights.

Part 2: The Art of Beer and Food Pairing

I n this part of the chapter, we'll delve into the fascinating world of beer and food pairing, exploring how different beer styles can complement and enhance a wide range of culinary delights. From classic pairings to unexpected combinations, the art of beer and food pairing offers endless opportunities for exploration, discovery, and enjoyment.

1. Understanding Flavor Interactions:

Beer and food pairing is all about understanding how different flavors, aromas, and textures interact with each other to create harmonious or contrasting flavor experiences. By considering the flavor profile of both the beer and the food, as well as their respective intensity, complexity, and balance, you can create pairings that elevate the dining experience and enhance the enjoyment of both.

2. Classic Pairings: Timeless Combinations

Some beer and food pairings have stood the test of time, becoming classic combinations that never fail to delight the palate. Here are a few examples of classic pairings:

• IPA and Spicy Foods:

The bold hop bitterness and citrusy aroma of an IPA (India Pale Ale) complement the heat and complexity of spicy foods, such as curries, tacos, and Thai dishes, while the carbonation helps to cleanse the palate and refresh the palate between bites.

• Stout and Chocolate Desserts:

The rich, roasty flavors of a stout, with notes of coffee, chocolate, and caramel, pair beautifully with rich and decadent chocolate desserts, such as brownies, chocolate cake, and flourless chocolate torte, creating a luxurious and indulgent flavor experience.

• Wheat Beer and Seafood:

The light, crisp, and effervescent character of a wheat beer, with hints of citrus, coriander, and spice, complements the delicate flavors of seafood, such as shrimp, crab, and oysters, enhancing the natural sweetness and brininess of the seafood.

3. Regional Pairings: Matching Beer with Local Cuisine

Beer and food pairing is also influenced by regional culinary traditions and ingredients, with certain beer styles being particularly well-suited to complementing the flavors and textures of local cuisine. Here are a few examples of regional pairings:

• Belgian Saison and French Cheese:

The fruity esters, spicy phenols, and effervescent carbonation of a Belgian Saison pair beautifully with a variety of French cheeses, such as Brie, Camembert, and Chevre, creating a delightful contrast of flavors and textures.

• German Lager and Pretzels:

The clean, crisp, and malt-forward character of a German Lager, such as Helles or Märzen, complements the salty and savory flavors of traditional German pretzels, enhancing the doughy sweetness and adding a refreshing counterpoint to the saltiness.

• American Pale Ale and Barbecue:

The caramel malt sweetness and moderate hop bitterness of an American Pale Ale balance the smoky, savory, and tangy flavors of barbecue dishes, such as ribs, brisket, and pulled pork, while the carbonation helps to cleanse the palate and refresh the palate between bites.

4. Experimental Pairings:

Pushing the Boundaries:

While classic and regional pairings offer tried-and-true combinations, beer and food pairing is also about experimentation and creativity, pushing the boundaries of flavor and imagination to create unexpected and memorable experiences. Here are a few examples of experimental pairings:

• Sour Beer and Pickled Vegetables:

The tart acidity and funky flavors of a sour beer, such as a Lambic or Gose, complement the tangy and briny flavors of pickled vegetables, such as pickles, kimchi, and sauerkraut, creating a vibrant and refreshing flavor contrast.

• Belgian Tripel and Spicy Sausages:

The fruity esters, spicy phenols, and effervescent carbonation of a Belgian Tripel harmonize with the rich and savory flavors of spicy sausages, such as chorizo, andouille, and bratwurst, while the alcohol warmth helps to balance the heat and intensity of the spices.

• Barrel-Aged Stout and Blue Cheese:

The bold, roasty flavors and velvety texture of a barrel-aged stout, with hints of whiskey, oak, and vanilla, pair beautifully with the creamy, tangy, and pungent flavors of blue cheese, such as Roquefort, Stilton, and Gorgonzola, creating a decadent and indulgent flavor experience.

By exploring the art of beer and food pairing, homebrewers can elevate the dining experience and create memorable moments that celebrate the diversity and versatility of beer. Whether it's classic combinations, regional pairings, or experimental experiments, the key is to trust your palate, embrace your creativity, and have fun exploring the endless possibilities of flavor and taste.

Chapter 6

Part 1: Beer and Community

In this part of the chapter, we'll explore the integral role that beer plays in fostering community, bringing people together, and creating shared experiences. From homebrew clubs and beer festivals to brewery taprooms and beer-centric events, the world of beer offers countless opportunities for connection, camaraderie, and celebration.

1. Homebrewing Clubs:

Fostering Creativity and Friendship:

Homebrewing clubs are vibrant communities of beer enthusiasts who come together to share their passion for brewing, exchange ideas, and support one another in their brewing endeavors. Whether it's swapping recipes, tasting each other's beers, or offering feedback and advice, homebrewing clubs provide a supportive and collaborative environment for brewers of all levels to learn, grow, and experiment.

• Brewing Workshops and Education:

Homebrewing clubs often organize brewing workshops, seminars, and educational events to help members improve their brewing skills, expand their knowledge of beer styles and ingredients, and stay up-to-date on the latest brewing techniques and trends. These events provide valuable opportunities for hands-on learning, mentorship, and networking within the brewing community.

• Competitions and Judging:

Many homebrewing clubs host competitions and judging events, where members can enter their beers for evaluation by certified beer judges and receive feedback on their brewing techniques, recipe formulations, and overall beer quality. Competitions are not only a fun and exciting way to showcase your brewing prowess but also an opportunity to learn from others, gain recognition for your achievements, and earn valuable feedback to improve your future brews.

• Social Gatherings and Events:

In addition to brewing-related activities, homebrewing clubs often organize social gatherings, potluck dinners, and beer-centric outings to foster friendship, camaraderie, and community spirit among members. These events provide opportunities for socializing, networking, and forming lasting friendships with fellow beer enthusiasts who share a passion for brewing and beer culture.

2. Beer Festivals:

Celebrating Diversity and Craftsmanship:

Beer festivals are lively and dynamic events that bring together breweries, beer lovers, and enthusiasts from around the world to celebrate the diversity and craftsmanship of beer. Whether it's a small local festival or a large-scale international event, beer festivals offer an unparalleled opportunity to sample a wide variety of beers, discover new breweries and beer styles, and immerse oneself in the vibrant and exciting world of craft beer.

• Tasting Sessions and Beer Gardens:

Beer festivals typically feature tasting sessions and beer gardens where attendees can sample a diverse selection of beers from different breweries, regions, and styles. From hop-forward IPAs and rich stouts to crisp lagers and funky sours, there's something for everyone to enjoy and explore at a beer festival.

• Brewery Booths and Meet-the-Brewer Sessions:

Many beer festivals feature brewery booths and meet-the-brewer sessions, where attendees can meet the faces behind their favorite breweries, learn about their brewing philosophies and techniques, and sample exclusive and limited-edition beers that are not available elsewhere. These interactions provide valuable insights into the brewing process, the stories behind the beers, and the passion and dedication of the brewers who create them.

• Educational Seminars and Panels:

Beer festivals often include educational seminars, panel discussions, and tasting workshops led by industry experts, brewers, and beer educators. These sessions cover a wide range of topics, including beer history, brewing science, beer and food pairing, sensory analysis, and sustainability, providing attendees with opportunities to deepen their knowledge and appreciation of beer while engaging with like-minded enthusiasts and experts in the field.

3. Brewery Taprooms:

Building Community and Connection:

Brewery taprooms are welcoming and inclusive spaces where beer lovers can gather to enjoy fresh, locally brewed beer in a convivial and relaxed atmosphere. Whether it's catching up with friends, meeting new people, or simply savoring a pint of your favorite brew, brewery taprooms serve as hubs of community activity and engagement, bringing people together around a shared love of beer.

• Tasting Flights and Brewery Tours:

Brewery taprooms often offer tasting flights and brewery tours, allowing visitors to sample a variety of beers, learn about the brewing process, and gain insight into the brewery's history, values, and ethos. Tasting flights provide an opportunity to explore different beer styles and flavors, while brewery tours offer behind-the-scenes glimpses into the inner workings of the brewery, from the brewhouse and fermentation tanks to the packaging and distribution facilities.

- Events and Special Releases:

Brewery taprooms frequently host events, release parties, and special releases to engage with their community and showcase their latest and greatest beers. Whether it's a themed tap takeover, a live music performance, or a bottle release of a highly anticipated beer, these events create excitement and buzz around the brewery, drawing in beer enthusiasts and fostering a sense of belonging and connection among patrons.

- Community Outreach and Engagement:

Brewery taprooms often engage in community outreach and philanthropic initiatives to give back to their local communities and support causes they care about. Whether it's sponsoring local events, fundraising for charitable organizations, or partnering with community groups and nonprofits, breweries play an active role in supporting and enriching the communities in which they operate, building goodwill and fostering a sense of pride and ownership among their patrons.

By actively participating in homebrewing clubs, attending beer festivals, and frequenting brewery taprooms, beer enthusiasts can immerse themselves in a vibrant and dynamic community of like-minded individuals who share a passion for brewing, beer culture, and community engagement. Whether it's brewing together, sharing stories and experiences, or simply enjoying a pint of beer with friends, the world of beer offers endless opportunities for connection, camaraderie, and celebration. In the next part of the chapter, we'll explore the future of beer, from emerging trends and innovations to the evolving landscape of the beer industry.

Part 2: The Future of Beer

In this part of the chapter, we'll peer into the crystal ball and explore the exciting future of beer, from emerging trends and innovations to the evolving landscape of the beer industry. As technology, consumer preferences, and cultural shifts continue to shape the world of beer, brewers and beer enthusiasts alike are poised to embrace new opportunities and challenges in the quest for great beer.

1. Craft Beer Revolution:

Embracing Diversity and Creativity:

The craft beer revolution shows no signs of slowing down, with brewers around the world continuing to push the boundaries of beer styles, flavors, and ingredients. From experimental hop varieties and innovative brewing techniques to unconventional flavor combinations and collaborative brews, craft brewers are embracing diversity and creativity in pursuit of unique and distinctive beers that captivate the imagination and tantalize the taste buds.

• Hazy IPAs and Juicy Pale Ales:

Hazy IPAs (India Pale Ales) and Juicy Pale Ales have surged in popularity in recent years, driven by their vibrant hop aromas, soft mouthfeel, and tropical fruit flavors. Brewers are experimenting with new hop varieties, hopping techniques, and adjuncts to create hazy and juicy beers that push the boundaries of traditional IPA and Pale Ale styles.

• Sour and Funky Beers:

Sour and funky beers, including Lambics, Goses, and Wild Ales, continue to captivate beer enthusiasts with their tart acidity, complex microbial character, and refreshing flavor profiles. Brewers are exploring mixed fermentation techniques, barrel aging, and fruit additions to create innovative and expressive sour and funky beers that challenge conventional notions of beer style and flavor.

• Low- and No-Alcohol Beers:

With an increasing focus on health and wellness, as well as changing consumer preferences for moderation and mindful drinking, low- and no-alcohol beers are gaining traction in the market. Brewers are experimenting with alternative ingredients, fermentation methods, and flavor profiles to create flavorful and satisfying beers that deliver the taste and experience of traditional beer without the alcohol content.

2. Technology and Innovation:

Brewing in the Digital Age:

Technology and innovation are transforming the way beer is brewed, consumed, and experienced, opening up new possibilities for brewers and consumers alike. From automated brewing systems and data-driven brewing processes to online beer communities and digital marketing strategies, technology is reshaping every aspect of the beer industry.

• Smart Brewing Equipment:

Advances in brewing technology, such as automated brewing systems, precision fermentation controls, and real-time monitoring sensors, are revolutionizing the brewing process, enabling brewers to achieve greater consistency, efficiency, and quality in their beers. Smart brewing equipment allows brewers to monitor and control every aspect of the brewing process, from mashing and lautering to fermentation and conditioning, with precision and accuracy.

● E-Commerce and Direct-to-Consumer Sales:

The rise of e-commerce platforms and direct-to-consumer sales channels has democratized access to craft beer, allowing consumers to purchase beer directly from breweries and online retailers with greater convenience and choice. E-commerce platforms offer a wide selection of craft beers from around the world, as well as exclusive releases, limited-edition collaborations, and subscription-based beer clubs that cater to beer enthusiasts seeking unique and hard-to-find brews.

● Virtual Beer Communities and Events:

In an increasingly digital world, virtual beer communities and events have emerged as vibrant hubs of beer culture and engagement, providing beer enthusiasts with opportunities to connect, learn, and share their passion for beer from the comfort of their own homes. Virtual beer tastings, brewery tours, and educational seminars allow participants to interact with brewers, beer experts, and fellow enthusiasts in real-time, fostering a sense of community and camaraderie in the digital space.

3. Sustainability and Social Responsibility:

Brewing for a Better Future:

Sustainability and social responsibility are becoming increasingly important considerations for breweries and consumers alike, as the beer industry grapples with environmental challenges, social inequalities, and ethical concerns. Breweries are taking proactive steps to reduce their environmental footprint, support local communities, and promote diversity, equity, and inclusion in the beer industry.

● Environmental Stewardship:

Breweries are implementing sustainable practices and initiatives to minimize their environmental impact, reduce resource consumption, and mitigate climate change. From investing in renewable energy sources and water conservation measures to implementing waste reduction and recycling programs, breweries are prioritizing environmental stewardship and sustainability in their operations.

• Community Engagement and Philanthropy:

Breweries are actively engaging with their local communities and supporting charitable causes through philanthropic initiatives, fundraisers, and community outreach programs. Whether it's sponsoring local events, partnering with nonprofit organizations, or donating a portion of sales to charitable causes, breweries are using their platform and resources to give back and make a positive difference in the communities they serve.

• Diversity, Equity, and Inclusion:

The beer industry is making strides towards greater diversity, equity, and inclusion, with breweries and beer organizations actively promoting diversity in their workforce, leadership, and marketing efforts. By fostering a more inclusive and equitable beer culture, breweries are creating opportunities for underrepresented groups, amplifying diverse voices, and building a stronger and more vibrant beer community for all.

As we look ahead to the future of beer, one thing is clear: the possibilities are endless. From new beer styles and brewing techniques to innovative technologies and sustainability initiatives, the beer industry is evolving and adapting to meet the changing needs and preferences of consumers while staying true to its roots of creativity, craftsmanship, and community. As beer enthusiasts, brewers, and industry stakeholders, we have an exciting journey ahead as we continue to explore, innovate, and celebrate the wonderful world of beer.

Final Words

If you enjoyed this book and feel that you gained a great deal of knowledge or even just honed the knowledge that you already possess, please leave a kind review.

Your reviews do multiple things for an author. They tell us that you actually enjoyed our work and they tell others on the Internet that they will enjoy it too!

Thank you so much and happy brewing!

Stay Safe!

Don't miss out!

Visit the website below and you can sign up to receive emails whenever That Beer Guy publishes a new book. There's no charge and no obligation.

https://books2read.com/r/B-A-QCQGB-JRXAD

BOOKS 2 READ

Connecting independent readers to independent writers.